DOCK·TO

The Dockfather

LOGAN LISLE

TEN PEAKS PRESS®
EUGENE, OR

Special thanks to Matt Lisle @coachsaysjokes
Cover design by Bryce Williamson
Interior design by Peter Gloege
Cover images © Byjeng; nameinfame / Getty Images

For bulk or special sales, please call 1-800-547-8979.
Email: CustomerService@hhpbooks.com

Dock Tok Presents...
The Dockfather

ISBN 978-0-7369-9137-7 (pbk.)
ISBN 978-0-7369-9138-4 (eBook)

Library of Congress Control Number: 2024949116

Printed in the United States
25 26 27 28 29 30 31 32 33 / VP / 10 9 8 7 6 5 4 3 2 1

I REPLACED MY ROOSTER

WITH A DUCK.

NOW I WAKE UP AT THE QUACK OF DAWN.

I like waiters.

They bring a lot to the table.

I LOST 20 PERCENT
OF MY COUCH.

OUCH.

I'M NOT SURE
WHICH IS THE BIGGEST
STATE IN THE US . . .

BUT ALASKA FRIEND.

My son said,
"Dad, can you put
my shoes on?"

I said, "I don't think
they're gonna fit me."

WHAT DO YOU CALL A PAPER AIRPLANE THAT CAN'T FLY?

STATIONERY.

I had a fish that could breakdance.

But only for twenty seconds.

And only once.

I BOUGHT A SCALE
OFF AMAZON.

IT'S IN THE MAIL . . .
I CAN'T WAIT.

What do you call
the world's greatest
hockey player who decides
not to play pickleball?

Wayne Regretsky.

TOMORROW MY SON AND I ARE GETTING NEW GLASSES.

AFTER THAT . . . ? WE'LL SEE.

What do you call
a polar bear
in the jungle?

Lost.

MY WIFE WAS BEGGING ME
TO STOP DOING
POLICE-RELATED PUNS.

I SAID, "ALRIGHT, I'LL GIVE IT ARREST."

Why can't you hear a pterodactyl using the bathroom?

The p is silent.

WHAT ARE BEARS
WITHOUT BEES?

EARS.

Toilet paper plays

an important roll

in my life.

HUMANS EAT MORE BANANAS
THAN MONKEYS . . .
WHICH MAKES SENSE . . .

I DON'T REMEMBER
THE LAST TIME I ATE A MONKEY.

Why do scuba divers
fall backward out of the boat?

Because if they fell forward,
they'd still be in the boat.

WHAT DO YOU CALL A WORLD-FAMOUS ROCK GROUP WITH FOUR GUYS WHO CAN'T SING?

MOUNT RUSHMORE.

What do you call it when Lincoln, Washington, Jefferson, and Roosevelt fall in poison ivy?

Mount Rashmore.

WHO WAS
THE LEAST GUILTY
AMERICAN PRESIDENT?

LINCOLN—HE WAS IN A CENT.

Five ants rented an apartment with another five ants.

Now they're tenants.

THIS YEAR,
I'M WALKING AWAY FROM
MY BANK ACCOUNT.

I'M GETTING RID OF ALL
THE NEGATIVE THINGS IN MY LIFE.

My daughter can't decide
if she wants to be
a hairdresser or a
short-story writer.

I guess she'll have to flip a coin:
heads or tales.

WHAT'S THE DIFFERENCE BETWEEN A DUCK AND GEORGE WASHINGTON?

ONE HAS A BILL ON ITS FACE,

ONE HAS A FACE ON A BILL.

If Abraham Lincoln
was still alive today,
what would he
be famous for?

Old age.

DO YOU KNOW WHAT'S WORSE THAN BITING INTO AN APPLE AND FINDING A WORM?

BITING INTO AN APPLE
AND FINDING HALF OF A WORM.

Does every sentence need to include a vegetable?

NOT NECE*CELERY*.

I WAS PLAYING CHESS
WITH MY FRIEND.
HE SAID, "LET'S MAKE THIS
MORE INTERESTING . . . "

SO WE STOPPED PLAYING CHESS.

I want to tell you about this girl who only eats plants.

You've probably never herbivore before.

I CAN'T BELIEVE
SOMEONE CAME INTO
MY HOUSE LAST NIGHT AND
STOLE ALL MY FRUIT.

I AM PEACHLESS.

I feel like people these days are just too judgmental.

I can tell just by looking at them.

YESTERDAY I SWALLOWED SOME FOOD COLORING.

THE DOCTOR SAYS I'M OKAY.
BUT I FEEL LIKE I DYED A LITTLE.

I think my phone
is broken.

Yesterday I pressed the home button . . .
and I was still at work.

TWO ARTISTS
HAD A FIGHT.

IT ENDED IN A DRAW.

An apple a day keeps
the doctors away.

At least if you throw it hard enough.

TODAY MY SON ASKED,
"CAN I HAVE A BOOKMARK?"

I BURST INTO TEARS.

ELEVEN YEARS OLD

AND HE STILL DOESN'T KNOW

MY NAME IS LOGAN.

To the person
who stole my dictionary—

I have no words.

I KNEW A MAN
WHO WAS ADDICTED
TO BRAKE FLUID.

HE SAID HE CAN STOP ANYTIME HE WANTS.

Every morning,
I announce to my family,
"I'm going jogging."
And then I don't go.

It's a running joke.

I TOLD MY BOSS,
"SORRY I'M LATE—
I WAS HAVING
COMPUTER PROBLEMS."

"HARD DRIVE?"

"NO, THE COMMUTE
WAS FINE . . .
IT WAS MY LAPTOP."

My wife was furious about my revolving door purchase.

Then she thought about it.
Eventually, she came around.

WHY WAS THE BABY JALAPEÑO SHIVERING?

HE WAS A LITTLE CHILE.

I ran outta toilet paper.

The *Times* are rough.

YOU WANNA KNOW
HOW YOU TEACH KIDS
ABOUT TAXES?

EAT 34 PERCENT OF THEIR ICE CREAM.

I was gonna tell you
a time-traveling joke.

But you guys didn't like it.

MY PSYCHIATRIST SAYS
I HAVE AN ISSUE
WITH REVENGE.

WE'LL SEE ABOUT THAT.

My kids put together
a PowerPoint presentation
on why we should
go to the water park.

It had several slides.

CAN FEBRUARY

MARCH?

NO . . . BUT APRIL MAY.

If athletes get
athlete's foot,
what do
astronauts get?

Missile toe.

I LOVE GOING OUTDOORS.

IT'S MUCH SAFER THAN GOING OUT WINDOWS.

Why was the pig covered in ink?

'Cause it lived in a pen.

PEOPLE SAY THEY PICK THEIR NOSE.

I FEEL LIKE I WAS JUST BORN WITH MINE.

I opened my birthday card
and loads of rice fell out.

I know who sent it. It was Uncle Ben.

WHAT DID THE DRUMMER NAME HIS DAUGHTERS?

ANNA ONE, ANNA TWO.

What do you call a short mother?

A mini-*mum*.

I'M SKEPTICAL ABOUT ANYONE THAT TELLS ME TO DO YOGA EVERY DAY.

IT SOUNDS LIKE A LITTLE BIT OF A STRETCH.

There are three types of people in this world.

Those who can count and
those who cannot count.

THIS MORNING, I SAW A LADY
TALKING TO HER CAT.
POOR WOMAN THOUGHT
THE CAT UNDERSTOOD HER.

I GOT HOME LATER AND
TOLD MY DOG—WE LAUGHED ABOUT IT.

I called
the paranoia hotline
this morning.

They said, "How did you get this number?"

WHAT DID THE RIGHT EYE SAY TO THE LEFT EYE?

BETWEEN YOU AND ME, SOMETHING SMELLS.

A perfectionist
walks into a bar.

Apparently, the bar wasn't set high enough.

TO THE PERSON
WHO STOLE MY BED:

I WON'T REST UNTIL I FIND YOU.

What did the pirate say when he turned 80?

"Aye matey."

IF YODA OWNED
A BUSINESS,
I BET IT WOULD
BE A TOYODA
DEALERSHIP.

I drove my Subaru Outback into a river.

Now it's a Scuba-ru.

DID YOU KNOW THAT NASA IS ABOUT TO LAUNCH A NEW MISSION TO APOLOGIZE TO ALIENS FOR EARTH POLLUTING SPACE?

IT'S CALLED "APOLLO-G."

My friend blocked me
on Facebook because I used
too many bird puns.

Toucan play at this game.

MY BOSS ASKED ME TO MAKE
A BUSINESS PRESENTATION.
HE SAID IT SHOULD START OFF
WITH A JOKE . . .

SO I PUT MY PAYCHECK ON THE FIRST SLIDE.

To whoever stole
my energy drinks:

I hope you can't sleep at night.

TO THE PERSON
WHO STOLE MY DIARY AND
THEN PASSED AWAY:

MY THOUGHTS ARE WITH YOUR FAMILY.

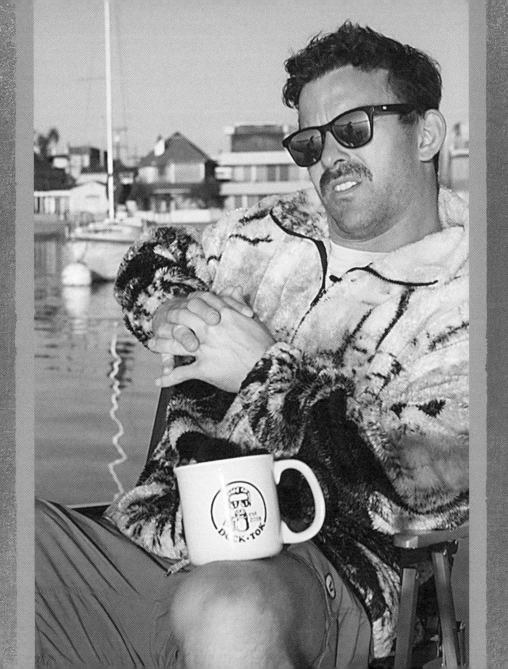

Yesterday I was on a plane
and the lunch choices
were white chicken meat
or German sausage.

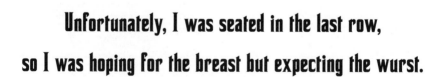

Unfortunately, I was seated in the last row,
so I was hoping for the breast but expecting the wurst.

A SHARK CAN SWIM
FASTER THAN ME,
BUT I CAN RUN
FASTER THAN A SHARK.

SO, IN A TRIATHLON, IT WOULD ALL
COME DOWN TO WHO'S THE BETTER CYCLIST.

Scientists got tired

of watching

the earth turn,

so after twenty-four hours,

they called it a day.

I SHOWED MY FRIEND
MY TOOL SHED AND
POINTED TO MY LADDER.

I TOLD HIM, "THAT'S MY STEPLADDER.
I NEVER KNEW MY REAL LADDER."

Jail might be
one word to you,

but to others it's a whole sentence.

TO WHOEVER STOLE
MY SELFIE STICK:

I HOPE YOU TAKE
A LONG LOOK AT YOURSELF.

What physical part of the computer never stops working?

The keyboard—it has two shifts.

WHAT HAPPENED WHEN NINETEEN GOT INTO A FIGHT WITH TWENTY?

TWENTY-ONE.

I just replaced my parents' bed with a trampoline.

They hit the roof.

I ATE A KID'S MEAL AT
MCDONALD'S TODAY.

HIS MOM GOT REALLY ANGRY.

I've been trying

to come up

with good jokes

about airplanes,

but I can't get any of them to land correctly.

WHAT DO YOU CALL
A FACTORY THAT JUST MAKES
OKAY PRODUCTS?

A SATISFACTORY.

I like to change
the "m" and the "n"
on people's keyboards
in the office.

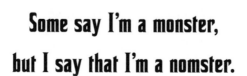

Some say I'm a monster,
but I say that I'm a nomster.

HOW DO YOU GET
ONE HUNDRED MATH TEACHERS
INTO A ROOM THAT
ONLY FITS NINETY-NINE?

YOU CARRY THE ONE.

What do you call men waiting in line to get a haircut?

A barbe-queue.

MY FRIEND SAID

HE'S A COMPULSIVE LIAR.

I DON'T BELIEVE HIM.

I saw a man going up a hill
with a trolley full of
four-leaf clovers, horseshoes,
and rabbits' feet.

I thought, "Wow, he's pushing his luck."

DO I ENJOY
MAKING JOKES
ABOUT JAIL?

GUILTY.

I sympathize
with batteries.

I'm not included in anything either.

I WAS GOING TO PROPOSE
TO MY GIRLFRIEND LAST NIGHT,
BUT MY DOG ATE THE RING.

NOW IT'S JUST A DIAMOND IN THE RUFF.

A polar bear walks
into a restaurant.
He tells the waiter,
"I'll have a burger . . .
and some fries."

The waiter asks, "What's up with the pause?"
The polar bear says, "I was born with them."

I HIRED A HANDYMAN
AND GAVE HIM
A TO-DO LIST.

WHEN I GOT HOME, ONLY ITEMS
ONE, THREE, AND FIVE WERE DONE.
IT TURNS OUT HE ONLY DOES ODD JOBS.

I'm trying
to organize a
hide-and-seek
tournament,

but good players are hard to find.

I TRIED TO GIVE MY FRIEND
AN APPLE THE OTHER DAY,
BUT HE SAID HE ONLY
LIKES PEARS.

SO, I GAVE HIM AN EXTRA APPLE.

If lightning hits an orchestra, who's most likely to get hit?

The conductor.

DID YOU KNOW THAT
INSURANCE COMPANIES
ARE WARNING CAMPERS
THAT IF YOUR TENT
IS STOLEN AT NIGHT,
YOU WON'T BE COVERED?

I went to the theater
to see a performance that
was all about puns.

It was a play on words.

I WAS DRIVING TO WORK
AND ROBBERS JUMPED
INTO MY CAR AND
STOLE EVERYTHING.

THEY WERE THE PIRATES
OF THE CAR-I-BE-IN.

Geology rocks.
But geography is
where it's at.

YOU WANNA KNOW

THE DIFFERENCE BETWEEN

ME AND A CALENDAR?

THE CALENDAR HAS DATES . . .

I can't believe
viruses and bacteria
would just invade
my body without
my permission.

It makes me sick.

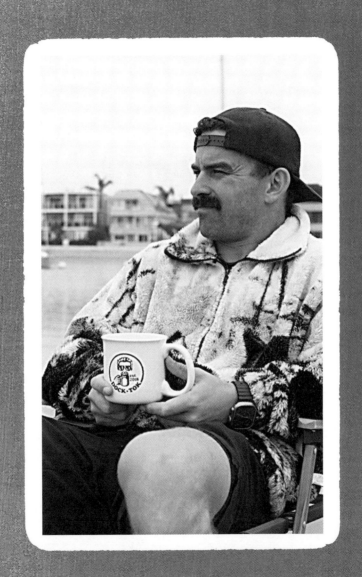

DID YOU HEAR
ABOUT THE GARDENER
THAT WENT CRAZY?

HE WAS HEARING VOICES IN HIS SHED.

My doctor told me that I'm suffering from paranoia.

Well, he didn't actually say that, but I could tell that's what he was thinking.

TWO GOLDFISH WERE
IN A TANK TOGETHER.

ONE SAID TO THE OTHER, "DO YOU KNOW
HOW TO DRIVE THIS THING?"

Yesterday I was washing the car with my son.

He said, "Dad, can't you just use a sponge?"

I HAVE AN INCREDIBLE GIFT
OF GUESSING WHAT'S
INSIDE A WRAPPED PRESENT.

IT'S A GIFT, I GUESS.

I asked my friend Sam

to sing a song

about the iPhone.

And then Samsung.

A FRIEND OF MINE
NAMED HIS DOG FIVE MILES . . .
SO HE COULD TELL EVERYBODY
HE WALKS FIVE MILES.

UNFORTUNATELY, YESTERDAY
HE RAN OVER FIVE MILES.

If you don't know what to talk about on a first date, talk about global warming.

It's a huge icebreaker.

WHAT DO YOU CALL
A RELUCTANT POTATO?

A HESI-TATER.

My friend just got done with the Dolly Parton diet.

It made Joe lean, Joe lean.

NEVER USE A
DOUBLE NEGATIVE.

THEY'RE A BIG NO-NO.

When we make pizza at home, my wife's job is to shred the cheese.

She's the grateist.

WHY DO ACTORS ALWAYS SAY, "BREAK A LEG"?

THEY ALWAYS WANNA BE IN A CAST.

IMAGINE IF AMERICANS SWITCHED FROM POUNDS TO KILOGRAMS OVERNIGHT.

THAT'D BE MASS CONFUSION.

My geography teacher asked me if I could name a country with no "r" in it.

I said Noway!

I RAN INTO A LAMPPOST YESTERDAY.

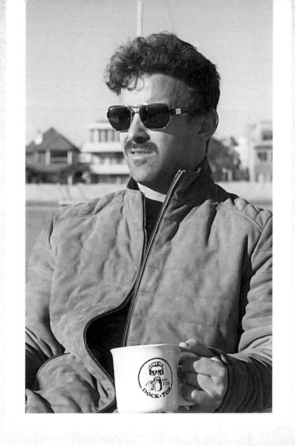

WELL, LUCKILY YOU ONLY
SUSTAINED LIGHT INJURIES.

I WAS AT A JOB INTERVIEW AND THE MANAGER HANDED ME A LAPTOP AND SAID, "I WANT YOU TO TRY AND SELL THIS TO ME." SO I PUT IT UNDER MY ARM, LEFT, AND WENT HOME. EVENTUALLY, HE CALLED AND SAID, "I WANT MY LAPTOP BACK."

I SAID, "$200 AND IT'S YOURS."

My doctor told me
I'm at risk for heart disease
'cause I eat too much sodium.

I took his advice with a pinch of salt.

MY SISTER
JUST HAD HER BABY.

I KNEW SHE HAD IT IN HER.

My kid asked me
what it's like to be a parent.

So, I woke him up at 2 a.m.
to tell him my sock came off.

YESTERDAY MY GPS
TOLD ME TO
TURN AROUND.

AFTER THAT, I COULDN'T SEE ANYTHING.

At the age of 65, my grandma started walking ten miles a day.

She's now 92 and we have no idea where she is.

I'M SO TERRIFIED TO ASK

MY WIFE TO CLEAN UP AFTER

MAKING BREAKFAST

THAT I'VE BEEN

WALKING ON EGGSHELLS

ALL DAY LONG.

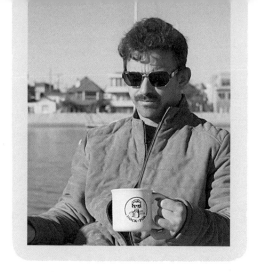

My wife lost our dog last night while she was making a salad.

If anybody Caesar, lettuce know.

THERE WAS A ROMAN EMPEROR WHO NEVER AGED PAST 19.

HIS NAME WAS CONSTANT-TEEN.

At the office barbecue
I grilled some rare steak
for our boss. And he said,
"I like it well done."

I said, "Well, thanks a lot."

HOW DO YOU PUT
A BABY ASTRONAUT
TO SLEEP?

YOU ROCKET.

I offered my elderly neighbor $20 for a ride on her stairlift.

I think she's gonna take me up on it.

I WAS AT THE OTHER
DOCKS AND ASKED A GUY,
"HOW MUCH DOES
THIS SHIP COST?"

HE SAID, "THIS SHIP? I GOT IT ON SAIL."

What did the Pink Panther say when he stepped on an ant?

Dead ant, dead ant, dead ant, dead ant, dead ant, dead ant, dead ant . . .

JUST HURT MY WRISTS DIGGING A HOLE BETWEEN TWO KOI PONDS.

THINK YOU HAVE

CARP-AL TUNNEL?

I ORDERED THIS BOOK ONLINE TITLED *HOW TO SCAM.*

IT'S BEEN SIX MONTHS NOW.

I HOPE IT ARRIVES SOON.

You bad at golf?

Join the club.

AN INVISIBLE MAN MARRIES

AN INVISIBLE WOMAN.

THE KIDS WERE NOTHING

TO LOOK AT EITHER.

My friend asked, "How does cloning work?"

I said, "That makes two of us."

HOW DOES NASA

ORGANIZE THEIR PARTIES?

THEY PLANET.

Do you know what the easiest shot to make in golf is?

Your fourth putt.

MY SON WAS CHEWING ON ELECTRICAL CORDS, SO I HAD TO GROUND HIM.

HE'S DOING BETTER CURRENTLY AND CONDUCTING HIMSELF PROPERLY.

My son asked me,
"Do trees poop?"

I said, "Where do you think
No. 2 pencils come from?"

MY GRANDFATHER SAID THAT
BACK IN THE DAY HE COULD
GO IN THE GROCERY STORE WITH
$2 IN HIS POCKET, COME OUT
WITH A LOAF OF BREAD, A DOZEN
EGGS, AND EVEN BUTTER.

HE SAID, "NOW THEY
HAVE CAMERAS EVERYWHERE."

I don't always tell Dad jokes,

but when I do, he laughs.

I WENT TO THE
TOY STORE AND ASKED
THE MANAGER WHERE THE
ARNOLD SCHWARZENEGGER
DOLLS WERE.

HE SAID, "AISLE B BACK."

Saying you did something at 5 a.m. makes you sound disciplined.

Saying you did something at 4 a.m.
just makes you sound irresponsible.

SEVEN DAYS

WITHOUT

A PUN

MAKES ONE

WEAK.

What's the best gift you could possibly give?

A broken drum. Nobody can beat that.

WHAT DID ONE OCEAN
SAY TO THE OTHER OCEAN?

NOTHING. THEY JUST WAVED.

What did one plate say to another plate?

Tonight, dinner's on me.

REST IN PEACE, BOILING WATER.

YOU WILL BE MIST.

Do you know
why you only make soup
with 239 beans?

'Cause one more would make it too-farty.

LAWYERS HOPE YOU GET SUED.

COPS HOPE YOU GET ARRESTED.

DOCTORS HOPE YOU GET SICK.

MECHANICS HOPE

YOUR CAR BREAKS DOWN.

BUT A THIEF JUST HOPES YOU PROSPER.

The police just knocked
on my door to tell me
that my dog was chasing
a kid on his bike.

I just shut the door.
My dog doesn't even have a bike.

YOU WANNA KNOW
THE DIFFERENCE BETWEEN
THE BLACK-EYED PEAS
AND CHICKPEAS?

THE BLACK-EYED PEAS CAN SING US A SONG,

CHICKPEAS CAN HUMMUS ONE.

My wife bet me $1,000 that I couldn't turn spaghetti into a car.

You should've seen her face when I drove pasta.

I WONDER
WHAT KIND OF TEA
RICH PEOPLE BUY.

PROPER TEA.

A storm blew off 25 percent of my roof last night.

Oof.

MY BIGGEST FEAR
IS BEING STUCK
IN A ROOM WITH SANTA.

I GUESS YOU COULD SAY
I'M CLAUS-TROPHOBIC.

Which celebrity
is always ready for cereal?

Reese with her spoon.

I ONCE
PULLED A MUSCLE
MINING FOR GOLD.

IT WAS A MINER INJURY.

Just so
everyone is clear,
I'm gonna put my
glasses on.

EVERY NEW YEAR'S EVE
I LOOK FORWARD TO A GOOD
SHOW AT TIMES SQUARE.

BUT YEAR AFTER YEAR,

THEY DROP THE BALL.

I asked Santa

for a globe this Christmas,

but I didn't get it.

Would've meant the world to me.

I WAS RUNNING
A DATING AGENCY
FOR CHICKENS.

BUT I WAS STRUGGLING
TO MAKE HENS MEET.

All I got for Christmas was a deck of sticky playing cards.

I'm having a hard time dealing with this.

MY DOCTOR TOLD ME I WAS GOING DEAF.

THAT NEWS WAS HARD TO HEAR.

My wife dropped
the laundry basket.

She's mad at me 'cause I just
stood there and watched it unfold.

I LOST MY WIFE'S
AUDIOBOOK.

NOW I'LL NEVER HEAR THE END OF IT.

I threw a boomerang
a couple years ago.

I now live in constant fear.

I'VE BEEN

INVITED TO JOIN

A SECRET SOCIETY.

I CAN'T TELL YOU HOW EXCITED I AM.

I can't understand
why my calculator
just stopped working.

It just doesn't add up.

I'M DONE BEING A

PEOPLE PLEASER . . .

IF EVERYONE'S OKAY WITH THAT!?

Logan Lisle

is the mastermind behind the hugely popular

Dock Tok series of online videos and the author

of the bestselling joke book *Dock Tok Presents . . .*

the Good, the Dad, and the Punny.

When he's not sitting by the lake sipping coffee

and trading dad jokes with his buddies,

he can be found at weddings all over the world

as a sought-after videographer or docked

at his new home in Phoenix, Arizona.